POCKET STUDY SKILLS

Series Editor: **Kate Williams,**
Oxford Brookes University, UK
Illustrations by Sallie Godwin

For the time-pushed student, the *Pocket Study Skills* pack a lot of advice into a little book. Each guide focuses on a single crucial aspect of study giving you step-by-step guidance, handy tips and clear advice on how to approach the important areas which will continually be at the core of your studies.

Published

14 Days to Exam Success (2nd edn)
Analyzing a Case Study
Blogs, Wikis, Podcasts and More
Brilliant Writing Tips for Students (2nd edn)
Completing Your PhD
Doing Research (2nd edn)
Doing Your Literature Review
Getting Critical (3rd edn)
How to Analyze Data
Managing Stress
Planning Your Dissertation (3rd edn)
Planning Your Essay (4th edn)
Planning Your PhD
Posters and Presentations

Reading and Making Notes (3rd edn)
Referencing, Understanding Plagiarism and
    Ethical AI (3rd edn)
Reflective Writing (2nd edn)
Report Writing (2nd edn)
Science Study Skills
Studying with Dyslexia (3rd edn)
Success in Groupwork (2nd edn)
Successful Applications
Time Management
Using Feedback to Boost Your Grades
Where's Your Evidence?
Writing for University (3rd edn)

POCKET STUDY SKILLS

Jeanne Godfrey

FROM ENGLISH LANGUAGE TEST TO UNIVERSITY SUCCESS

BLOOMSBURY ACADEMIC
LONDON · NEW YORK · OXFORD · NEW DELHI · SYDNEY

BLOOMSBURY ACADEMIC
Bloomsbury Publishing Plc, 50 Bedford Square, London, WC1B 3DP, UK
Bloomsbury Publishing Inc, 1359 Broadway, New York, NY 10018, USA
Bloomsbury Publishing Ireland, 29 Earlsfort Terrace, Dublin 2, D02 AY28, Ireland

BLOOMSBURY, BLOOMSBURY ACADEMIC and the Diana logo are trademarks of Bloomsbury Publishing Plc

First published in Great Britain 2026

Copyright © Jeanne Godfrey, 2026

Jeanne Godfrey has asserted her right under the Copyright, Designs and Patents Act, 1988, to be identified as Author of this work.

Cover design: Jade Barnett

A catalogue record for this book is available from the British Library.

Library of Congress Cataloging-in-Publication Data
Names: Godfrey, Jeanne author
Title: From English language test to university success / Jeanne Godfrey.
Description: London ; New York : Bloomsbury Academic, 2026. | Includes bibliographical references and index. |
Summary: "This short and pithy guide helps readers to understand the differences between English language tests and university-level work. It covers the study and language skills directly connected to using (English) language successfully in an academic context. It also covers critical thinking, disciplinary knowledge, styles and genres, useful skills for reading, making notes, writing assessments (particularly use of language) understanding lectures and seminars, and speaking in seminars"– Provided by publisher.
Identifiers: LCCN 2025041213 (print) | LCCN 2025041214 (ebook) | ISBN 9781350517141 paperback | ISBN 9781350517165 epub | ISBN 9781350517158 pdf
Subjects: LCSH: Study skills | College students | English language–Examinations | English language–Study and teaching (Higher) | cademic achievement
Classification: LCC LB1049 .G646 2026 (print) | LCC LB1049 (ebook)
LC record available at https://lccn.loc.gov/2025041213
LC ebook record available at https://lccn.loc.gov/2025041214

ISBN: PB: 978-1-350-51714-1
              ePDF: 978-1-350-51715-8
              eBook: 978-1-350-51716-5

Series: Pocket Study Skills

Typeset by Integra Software Services Pvt. Ltd.

Printed and bound in India

For product safety related questions contact productsafety@bloomsbury.com.

To find out more about our authors and books visit www.bloomsbury.com and sign up for our newsletters.

Contents

Introduction

Who this book is for:

- anyone who has taken or will take an English language test for entry to university.

This book:

- explains and demonstrates the differences between English language test tasks and what you need to do for university study
- uses real academic sources and student writing as examples
- suggests ways you can prepare for the language demands of your degree course
- shows you what tutors are looking for in student assignments
- suggests ways you can develop your disciplinary knowledge, your critical and creative thinking skills and your use of academic language to produce top-level university work.

English language tests (ELTs) are expertly researched and are excellent at testing what they are designed to test. They assess language proficiency over a range of language skills that are an important foundation for academic work. Getting the ELT score you need for your university course indicates that you have a great deal of valuable English language ability.

But . . .

these tests are designed to assess your general English language proficiency before going to university, not to help you succeed once you get there. In addition, the tests are designed for a global audience and so cannot rely on you having any knowledge of particular academic subjects. Finally, ELTs need to be short (anything from about one to three hours) and done under exam conditions. Inevitably then, there are many differences between what you are required to do in an English language entry test and what you will need to do once you start your academic course.

A summary of the differences

	What you need to do in an English language test	**What you need to do at university**
Topics	Understand topics that are usually familiar and that focus on concrete events, processes and practices.	Understand topics that are subject-specific, often including abstract and/or theoretical concepts.
Vocabulary (Chapter 3)	Show you can use a range of general academic vocabulary.	Understand and use both general and subject-specific academic vocabulary to communicate clearly.
Listening (Chapter 4)	Listen to several very short passages on non-academic or semi-academic topics.	Listen to live or recorded lectures, presentations and podcasts of varying lengths, from ten minutes to one hour.
Speaking (Chapter 4)	Participate in short one-to-one discussions on familiar topics.	Participate in a variety of group situations such as discussions (seminars, tutorials, debates), giving presentations and presenting posters.

Written tasks (Chapter 5)	Complete short writing tasks on general and/or familiar topics, using basic paragraph structure, signposting language and logical order.	Complete subject-specific assignments of different lengths, styles and types, according to level of study and discipline.
Selecting source material (Chapter 6)	You do not have to select source material.	Search for and select source material as a fundamental part of academic work.
Reading and making notes (Chapter 7)	Answer short comprehension questions or describe the content of short texts on general and/or familiar topics. Note-taking is not usually tested.	Analyse and evaluate subject-specific, often quite complex texts. Make notes according to your reading purpose as a key part of academic work.
Developing original ideas (Chapter 8)	The ability to develop your own ideas is not tested.	Develop your own informed ideas and position on subject-specific issues.
Using source material (Chapter 9)	Produce short descriptive summaries and/or paraphrase of relatively simple texts. Describe simple visual data. Full and clear source acknowledgement is not tested.	Analyse and evaluate sources you have selected and use them in your work to support your own arguments. Fully acknowledge all sources.

	What you need to do in an English language test	**What you need to do at university**
Communicating your ideas clearly (Chapter 10)	Communicate information and views on a familiar topic. Use a semi-formal and/or journalistic writing style.	Communicate a developed academic argument using source material to support your points. Convey your ideas clearly and precisely using formal (academic) but non-complex language.

 ## So, what can you do to bridge the gap?

1 Be aware of the differences

Try not to worry about all the differences summarized above. Just realizing that there *are* differences, and having at least some idea of what these are, will help you enormously at university and will mean that you are more prepared than many other students.

One important thing to realize is that you may need to 'unlearn' some of the things you practised for your English test. For example, at university you will need to question rather than describe things, use a more precise writing style, and be aware that you are being assessed on the content of what you say rather than on the range of grammatical forms and vocabulary you use to say it.

2 Do some preparation

Few students are experts in their academic discipline or in using 'academic language' before they start their course, and most students find university work difficult. This challenge can be even greater at postgraduate level, in part because the gap between English language test tasks and the linguistic demands of higher-level study is bigger than at undergraduate level. So, doing as much preparation as you can before you start your course will go a long way to helping you succeed once you get there.

Ways you can prepare include:

- reading this book and doing some of the things suggested in Chapters 1 to 3
- continuing to develop your general English proficiency. The higher your level of general English language proficiency, the more likely you are to succeed at university (Murray, 2016).

Note that the English language test scores universities require are usually set at the lowest level of language proficiency needed to start the course. So, if your ELT score is at or only just above the required level, it is worth considering postponing your course start date by six months to a year. This will give you time to further develop your general language proficiency and your academic subject vocabulary.

Key points

1 Be aware of the main differences between English language test tasks and university work so that you adapt more quickly once you start your course.
2 Learn a bit about your academic subject and its key terms before you start university.
3 Many students find academic work difficult at first, including those who have English as their first or main language.

Your general academic context

It's important to understand how your tutors will expect you to approach university study. Your tutors will want you to:

1 Use current knowledge to create new knowledge

Universities are places where current knowledge is gathered, shared and analysed in order to develop new knowledge. For something to count as knowledge in an academic sense it must be supported by evidence and/or logical argument. Knowledge is viewed as provisional, in other words as 'only what we know now', and even subject experts realize that they don't have all the answers. Finally, knowledge is seen as

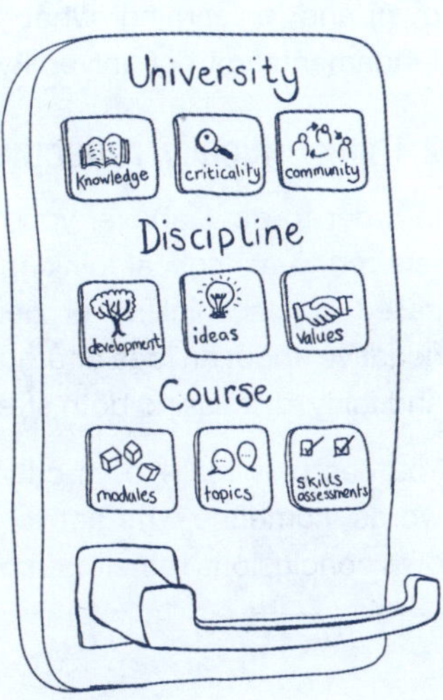

something that should always be open to analysis and challenge, and to do this we need to know where it comes from.

So, your university tutors will want you to question knowledge and viewpoints rather than learn facts or try to find 'correct' answers. Questioning ideas (including your own) and 'unlearning' what you think you know can feel uncomfortable, but it is a fundamental part of university study.

2 Think critically, reflectively, independently and creatively

In order to do 1 above, you need to think in an analytical and reflective way – often referred to as 'critical thinking'. Having a questioning approach is a key part of what's called critical thinking or being critical. 'Being critical' here does not mean being negative about an idea or argument – it means analysing and evaluating something fully and fairly, discussing both strengths and weaknesses. (See also Chapter 9, pp. 89–91.)

You can only really be a critical thinker if you are also an independent one; in other words, someone who actively seeks out ideas, questions things and arrives at their own conclusions rather than being told what to think. Importantly, by approaching your subject in a critical way, you will find that you *automatically* create your own unique insights, ideas and solutions.

3 Become an active member of your academic community

By doing 1 and 2 above, you will start to become someone who thinks about, questions and creates knowledge and ideas in your field. In other words, you will become part of your academic community, made up of the students and staff on your course, your faculty, your university and beyond. Try to be an active member of this community and seek out discussion and feedback from the students, researchers and experts around you.

Keep these three points in mind as you go through the rest of this book.

Your disciplinary context

You also need to think about the specific context of your subject. Different disciplines (and even the sub-disciplines within them) will often have different ways of thinking about knowledge and will value different key skills. As an example of this, here is a summary of ways of thinking and valued skills in five different disciplines.

Discipline	Ways of thinking and valued skills
Chemical Science	**Ways of thinking** Key aim is to understand the natural and physical world. Things in the world can be measured and tested, but we can never assume we have the best or correct answer as there can always be new and/or conflicting data. Data can only be interpreted rather than presenting a 'universal truth' and we can only disprove rather than prove, ideas. We need to understand the assumptions, issues and complexities behind 'facts' and 'answers'. **Valued skills** Select, understand and evaluate relevant studies in order to highlight current controversies. Compare and group sources in order to identify common themes and knowledge gaps. Analyse data using scientific tools and interpret data in order to draw your own conclusions. Produce persuasive arguments supported by relevant information.

Discipline	Ways of thinking and valued skills
Nursing	**Ways of thinking** Reality can be measured and tested, but we must always be open to new and/or conflicting data. We investigate the world in a realistic and pragmatic way in order to provide the best care, using the best data we have at the moment. Patients are free and responsible agents and should be able to choose how they are treated. **Valued skills** Draw together, analyse and critically evaluate information. Communicate effectively with individuals, groups and organizations. Produce accurate records and make informed decisions. Explain and justify practice by using relevant theory and data.

Discipline	Ways of thinking and valued skills
Art and Design	**Ways of thinking** To some extent we construct reality in our minds, and there are no absolute definitions of concepts such as 'art' or 'beauty'. Art can be both an interpretation and reflection of, reality. Social and personal contexts and relationships impact our interpretations of art. **Valued skills** Analyse and evaluate a work of art in terms of the artist's technique and intended meaning. Discuss a work's cultural and social significance. Give personal and descriptive reactions supported by relevant theory, ideas and examples. Create your own interpretations of artwork, even if they go against authoritative convention.

Discipline	Ways of thinking and valued skills
Civil Engineering	**Ways of thinking** The physical environment exists, and our key aim is to find the best engineering solutions to problems within it. We should consider relevant philosophical issues (such as the subjectivity of data or how society creates meaning in the world) so that we can find the best engineering solutions. **Valued skills** Identify and propose solutions to real-life problems, using relevant theory and practice. Conduct detailed analysis of case study scenarios and real situations. Apply disciplinary knowledge to problems and recommend solutions and future actions.

Discipline	Ways of thinking and valued skills
Maths	**Ways of thinking** There is a range of philosophical approaches in mathematics, including the views that maths exists outside the rest of 'reality', that only maths truly exists, and that maths is an art form. **Valued skills** Show the truth of mathematical statements via logic. Demonstrate awareness of the implications of mathematical statements. Use deductive argument to test existing theories. Combine ideas under a common model.

# So, what can you do to bridge the gap?

Investigate the ways of thinking and values of your discipline

Ways of doing this include:

1 reading your course and module descriptions – what do they say about approaches to knowledge, schools of thought, approaches to learning and key skills? What types of things do the module descriptions and assessment criteria say will be assessed?

2 paying attention to the instructional verbs and nouns you come across when reading your course description (examples of these are *analyse*, *argue*, *debate*, *define*, *evaluate*, *observe*, *record*, *reflect*, *relate*, *solve* and *test*). Make sure you understand what these words mean.

3 reading an introductory book or online article that summarizes the history of your subject. Find out how it has developed its knowledge and ideas, and who has been important in this process. Learn a bit about the current viewpoints and controversies within the field.

4 reflecting on everything you have found out – you might find that you have developed or changed some of the ideas you have about your subject and about how it approaches and investigates knowledge. If you are doing a course that involves more than one discipline, reflect on the similarities and differences between them.
5 reflecting on what interests and surprises you most about your subject. You might find it useful to discuss your thoughts with friends and family, with students on campus, via online student groups or by starting your own academic blog.

Key points

1 At university, learning is not about remembering facts and finding correct answers but about a continual process of questioning and reflecting on current knowledge in order to create new knowledge.
2 Challenging and perhaps unlearning some of your views about things can be difficult, even unpleasant, but is an essential part of higher learning.
3 Different disciplines do things differently, so find out about the nature of your subject.

What you need to do in an English language test	What you need to do at university
Show you can use a range of general academic vocabulary.	Understand and use both general and subject-specific academic vocabulary to communicate clearly.

English language tests require that you understand and use a range of words that can be used across disciplines; words such as *capacity*, *curb*, *endorse*, *fluctuate*, *however*, *moreover* and *scarce*. This category of words is referred to as common academic, general academic or sub-technical vocabulary. At university you will need to continue developing this area of word knowledge and also use an increasing amount of what is called disciplinary, specialized or technical vocabulary.

Examples of disciplinary terms:

Nursing:	*nursing enquiry, ambulatory care, triage*
Journalism:	*bounce rate, lede, standfirst*
Cultural anthropology:	*animatism, agnatic, levirate*
Maths:	*formalism, modal, natural number*

Using words precisely is essential for university-level work. As an example, below are four common academic words you might already know:

1 challenge (v, n)
2 cite (v)
3 generally (adv)
4 imply (v)

. . . and here are four sentences from student assignments in which these words have been used in a 'nearly but not quite right' way, making the meaning of the sentence unclear or incorrect.

A suggestion for a correct word choice is given in brackets at the end of each sentence.

1 Gibson (2024) *raises the challenges* facing the development of the IZ drug trials. (*discusses the challenges*)
2 As Feynman (2005) *cites*: 'If you can't explain something . . . you haven't really understood'. (*states*)
3 The population of Argentina is *generally* 46.5 million. (*approximately*)
4 Mathematics is an *implied* part of studying chemistry. (*explicit*)

 FROM ENGLISH LANGUAGE TEST TO UNIVERSITY SUCCESS

Common causes of using words imprecisely or incorrectly include:

- understanding a word well enough when reading but not well enough to *use* it correctly
- using the right word but making a mistake with the words that come before or after it.

 ## So, what can you do to bridge the gap?

You probably have good vocabulary learning strategies already, but here are a few suggestions you might want to add to your current methods:

1 Read as much and as widely as possible.
2 Note down words in an organized way. It is useful to note down new words in the context of a whole sentence.
3 Focus on learning the most useful words, both common academic and disciplinary. These will be the words you keep coming across in your course and module descriptions and in your subject reading. Note that online subject dictionaries and lists of key terms are useful but try to avoid using long word lists to learn new vocabulary; it's better to do so in the context of reading, writing and talking about your subject.

4 Understand new words properly. Use an English–English dictionary to check the meaning of a word and to find out:

- what *type* of thing is it (e.g. a concept, process, technique, philosophy, ideology, organism)
- other forms of the word (noun, verb and adjectival forms)
- key grammar points
- other words commonly used with the key word
- whether the word has different/special meanings in different disciplines.

As an example of the types of things you need to know, below are some notes for the word *consider*.

Noun: *Consideration of* this issue is . . . We need to *keep* the issue *under consideration*.
Adjective: A *considerable amount of* research
Verb: *We need to consider* this issue
Adverb: There is *considerably more* / This has improved *considerably*
Special disciplinary meaning: In contract law, *a consideration* is a benefit which must be bargained for between parties and is the reason for entering into a contract.

- Prompt a Gen AI tool to break down or simplify definitions of disciplinary concepts (but check the output against a reliable subject glossary or list). Then use some of these words to write your own definitions.

 FROM ENGLISH LANGUAGE TEST TO UNIVERSITY SUCCESS

- Practise using words in various ways, for example by using them in sentences, using them to write definitions of key concepts, writing down your thoughts and ideas, and writing short summaries of texts you read.
- Practise pronouncing and using words in speech. Use them to talk about key concepts in your subject.

Key points

1 In your assignments, don't suddenly try to use lots of words you don't fully understand. It's better to use the vocabulary you already have and to learn and use new words at a steady pace.

2 Learn new words because they are useful, not because you think they will make your work look 'academic' or 'complicated'.

3 Keep developing both your general and subject-specific academic vocabulary in an active way, using words in both speech and writing.

Listening

What you need to do in an English language test	What you need to do at university
Listen to very short passages on topics that are either: ▶ non-academic, e.g. plot summary of a novel ▶ semi-academic (not subject-specific), e.g. a tutor discussing assignment deadlines ▶ subject-specific but familiar, e.g. The Solar System. The speech in the passages is relatively slow and the speakers usually have standard accents.	Listen to live or recorded lectures, presentations and podcasts varying in length from five or ten minutes to an hour. Topics are subject-specific. The lecturer's speaking style might be slow or fast and often unique to them in some way. Their accent will often be unfamiliar to the listeners.

# So, what can you do to bridge the gap?

1 Research the topics and vocabulary of your lectures

Although listening practice on any topic will help develop your general proficiency, one of the most effective ways of preparing for your university lectures is to *get specific*. In Chapter 3, I suggested reading the titles and descriptions of your core modules and finding out the meanings and pronunciation of key terms. Do the same thing for your lectures – find out your lecture titles as early as possible and research the meanings and pronunciation of key words; this will help you recognize them when you hear them, and so help you understand the lecture as a whole. You can also search for online lectures and/or presentations on topics that are *as close as possible* to those of your lectures.

An example of finding out about lecture vocabulary:

Course title: BSc in Biological Sciences

Year 1 Core module – Biochemistry and Molecular Biology

The module description gives several lecture titles. One lecture is titled 'The relationship between protein structure and function'. Reading the lecture description and using the lecture title to search online gives key vocabulary that will probably be used in the lecture, for example: *enzyme catalysis*, *fold*, *motif*, *polypeptide* and *quaternary*.

2 Research the speaking styles of your lecturers

Your lecturers probably won't have the standard accents and speaking styles you encountered in your English language exam. They might have accents and speaking styles that are unfamiliar to you and/or might speak quickly. Some lecturers might not structure their talk clearly.

Knowing a bit about your lecturer's speaking style before a lecture (or even before your course starts) can be useful. You can sometimes find out who will be giving your lectures by looking at your module descriptions, course handbook, and the 'staff information', 'our team', 'your tutors' or 'who we are' sections of your department website. Once you know the name of a tutor you can look at the university website and other online platforms to see if they have published any lectures, talks or podcasts you can listen to.

An example of finding out about lecturers' speaking style:

Course title: BSc in Biological Sciences

Year 1 Core module – Biochemistry and Molecular Biology

The bottom of the module webpage gives the name of the module leader. The page also states that the course is run by the School of Biosciences within the

Faculty of Life Sciences. On the Faculty of Life Sciences webpage there is a 'meet our experts' section, giving brief biographies of module lecturers and links to short introduction videos by each one. In addition, on YouTube there are lectures and presentations by several of these lecturers.

3 Prepare for each lecture

Before the lecture:
- brainstorm what you know about the topic
- do the required pre-lecture reading
- check the meaning and pronunciation of key terms
- read the lecture title, handouts and slides, and use the main headings to prepare a simple note-making template. At the top of the template put your own questions and thoughts on the topic
- think about *why* you are being asked to watch the lecture; for example, is it to explain a new concept, develop your understanding of a concept you already know, critically evaluate a concept or to help you see links between concepts?

During the lecture:
- listen and engage rather than reading the handout or making lots of notes. Use your prepared template to keep your own questions in mind as you listen, and

to write brief notes (if you need to) and your own thoughts and questions to investigate later

- don't panic if you don't understand what's being said in a face-to-face lecture. Relax, breath, and wait for the next obvious point at which to start listening again.

Things to pay particular attention to:

- the start of the lecture when the speaker usually gives a content outline and states key points
- the end of the lecture when the speaker usually summarizes the most important points
- the lecturer raising their voice and/or speaking more slowly to emphasize key points
- signposting language (e.g. *firstly*, *moving on*, *the next point*, *to sum up*) used to structure the lecture
- whether the lecturer is giving a key point, a fact, a description, an explanation, an example or an opinion
- words that qualify a statement (e.g. *always*, *often*, *rarely*) and words that give a negative, such as *no*, *not*, *never*, *fails to* or *neglects to*.

After the lecture:

- take a step back and reflect on *why* you have been asked to listen to this lecture
- review, amend and add to any notes you made. Add date and time and a key to any abbreviations you have used. Check that you can see which information is from the lecturer and which are your own comments. Underline key points, correct any errors and look up any words you don't understand
- critically review the lecture and write down your own summary, evaluation and ideas. What follow-up questions would you like to ask? What further research and references do you want to chase up? How does the content relate to the rest of the module and your course in general? What was said in the lecture that really interested you, and why?

If a lecture is face-to-face, sit towards the front of the room – it's easy to become distracted and disengaged when sitting near the back.

Many students (including fluent English speakers) find some lectures hard to understand. If you find a lecture difficult, talk to the other students about it – some of them probably feel the same. You will usually be able to use lecture recordings and transcripts to help you, and if there is still something important you don't understand, contact the lecturer to ask for clarification.

Be aware that although listening to online resources such as TED talks is good general listening practice, they are usually too slow and general to be effective preparation for understanding your specific lectures.

Speaking

What you need to do in an English language test	What you need to do at university
Participate in short, one-to-one discussions. Talk for about three to five minutes on familiar topics such as transport in your city or a memorable experience.	Participate in a variety of speaking events, such as group discussions, seminars, individual or joint presentations, academic poster presentations and one-to-one personal tutor meetings.

You will probably need to participate in a range of different speaking components on your course, both formal (e.g. presentations or seminars) and informal (e.g. working with a lab partner, discussing ideas over lunch). Importantly, most of these speaking situations require you to:

   FROM ENGLISH LANGUAGE TEST TO UNIVERSITY SUCCESS

- listen, engage with and respond to what the other participants are saying
- take a critical approach. This involves thinking deeply about the topic, preparing informed questions and remaining open to changing your views as the discussion develops.

 ## So, what can you do to bridge the gap?

Before delivering a presentation

Know what to expect:

- watch some online academic presentations and, if possible, speak to students who have experience of presenting.

Prepare well:

- understand and become familiar with your topic
- check how to pronounce your key vocabulary
- have a clear main message that you can express simply and clearly in your own words
- think about your audience – what will they want (and not want) to hear about?
- have a clear and logical presentation structure
- create visuals that your audience will be able to read and understand.

Practise:
- delivering your presentation and check your timing
- speaking fairly slowly and clearly with plenty of short pauses at appropriate points.

Before a group seminar or discussion

Prepare your thoughts on the topic

Make sure you understand the key terms and ideas and do the required reading. Reflect on what you have read – what are your views on the topic? How have these been informed by your reading? What is your evaluation of the texts? What questions do you have?

Prepare what you want to say

Prepare and practise out loud what you think you will want to say, even if it is just one idea, critique or question. You can use a Gen AI tool to practise and gain confidence speaking about a topic (but check whether you need to declare doing so, particularly if it is for a formal assessment).

Prepare to keep an open mind and to be authentic

Prepare to listen, respond and keep an open mind. The point of most seminars and discussions is to develop your understanding of the topic, not to have a fixed viewpoint. Also remember that in the seminar your tutor will want to know what you really think, not what you think they want to hear.

FROM ENGLISH LANGUAGE TEST TO UNIVERSITY SUCCESS

Do some pronunciation practice

Make sure you are confident on how to pronounce key words. You should also check how to pronounce author surnames, as these are used to refer to sources.

For example:

Sharma 2020 suggests that . . .
I'm not sure what Briggs and Lia mean when they say . . .
Why do you think Nowak, Shore and Patel argue that . . .?
Data from Veenhoven et al.'s 2024 study shows that . . .

During a group seminar or discussion

Your tutor is interested in:

- what you think
- that you are developing informed points of view, criticisms and questions about the topic
- that you are listening and engaging, able to admit a change of view as the discussion develops.

Your tutor is *not* interested in:

- how many words you know
- whether you can use a range of discussion phrases or complex sentences
- whether you have perfect grammar (you just need to be able to communicate clearly).

Keep it simple

Try to convey your points using clear, simple language. You do not need to use all the 'seminar/discussion phrases' you might have learnt for your English language test. Such phrases are too long for real-life discussions and seminars, and your tutor is not interested in whether you can use them or not.

So, in real academic seminars and discussions you can just use the same short phrases repeatedly.

For example:

To disagree with someone:	*Yes, but . . .*	*Ok, but . . .*	*You have a point but . . .*
To agree with someone:	*Yes.*	*Good point.*	*I agree.*
To start/make a new point:	*I think that . . .*	*An interesting point is . . .*	
To ask a question:	*Why/When/What/Where is/Does/Do you think . . .?*		

It is normal for both students and tutors to ask someone to explain or repeat something so don't be afraid to ask for clarification. Useful phrases for this are: *Sorry, could you explain/say/repeat that again please?*

It's never too late to contribute

If you feel you were too quiet in the discussion and there was a point or question you wanted to contribute but didn't, speak to your tutor afterwards or send them a brief email telling them what you wanted to say – they will be interested to know. If the next group discussion is on the same topic you can also convey your point then, using phrases such as *'I forgot/meant/wanted to say last time that . . .'*

Key points

1 The lectures, videos and podcasts you are asked to listen to on your course are important. They are where your tutors explain, develop, question and bring to life key areas of knowledge in your field – make the most of them.
2 Research the key vocabulary of your lecture topics, including how to pronounce key words.
3 Prepare to listen, respond, be open-minded and be authentic.
4 Your tutors are interested in knowing what you think.

What you need to do in an English language test (writing tasks)	What you need to do at university (written assignments)
Complete short writing tasks on general and/or familiar topics.	Complete subject-specific assignments of different lengths, styles and types, according to level of study and discipline.
Use basic paragraph structure, signposting language and logical order.	Example assignment types: report, academic poster, discursive essay, reflective journal, annotated bibliography, literature review.
Describe simple data and text, state advantages/disadvantages and/or cause and effect and use these to justify your viewpoint.	Analyse and evaluate source material as part of developing an argument. At higher levels you often create your own research question.
Task timings are short, for example, three minutes to read a short passage and 20 minutes or less to write a short answer.	Some courses have exams, but you often need to develop and complete an assignment in your own time over a period of weeks or months.
The word limit is usually 200–300 words, up to a maximum of 700 words in some ELTs.	Shorter assignments are often 1,000–2,000 words and longer ones 5,000+ words.

You will probably have to complete some written assignments on your course. The most important difference between ELT writing tasks and written university assignments is that at university you need to write less about the *what* and more about the *why*.

So, what can you do to bridge the gap?

1 For each assignment check that you understand the following aspects:

- **type:** there are different assignment types and sub-types, each requiring a (slightly) different style, content and structure. There are, for example, different types of essays (e.g. argumentative, discursive, expository, reflective) and different types of reports (e.g. research, lab, executive)
- **purpose:** read the learning outcomes and reflect on why your tutor has set the assignment
- **title and instructions/brief:** (see 2 below)
- **marking criteria:** ① The phrases used in these can sometimes be vague or ambiguous, for example: *full range of sources/integrated presentation of sources/give a critical argument/evaluative arguments/publishable quality*. Read the marking criteria carefully and ask your tutor for clarification if there is anything you don't understand.

Below is a summary of some written assignment types and what you would be expected to do in each one.

Assignment type	What you need to do
Case study essay	Show understanding of the issue and identify and/or propose solutions to a problem in a real-life situation, using relevant theory and practices.
Argumentative essay	Make a statement that gives your perspective on the issue and then present a logical series of points and evidence that supports your argument and persuades the reader of its validity.
Reflective essay	Critically reflect on the experience/piece of practice, using relevant theory and then determine improved future practice and actions.
Written visual analysis	Analyse and evaluate a work of art in terms of the artist's technique and intended meaning. Discuss its cultural and social significance.
Mathematical proof	Examine and show (rather than accept) the truth of a mathematical statement. Show your understanding and demonstrate awareness of implications.

 FROM ENGLISH LANGUAGE TEST TO UNIVERSITY SUCCESS

Assignment type	What you need to do
Laboratory report	Record detailed observations and findings and then interpret your data. Address the *how* and *why* of your data, rather than making a prediction (hypothesis) and then looking for evidence to support it.
Literature review (As either a section within an essay/report or as a stand-alone assignment)	Select and show your understanding of relevant sources and how they connect to each other and to the assignment questions. Compare and group these sources to identify common themes and research gaps and to 'tell the background story' of the topic or issue.
Annotated bibliography	Give full reference details for the sources you have read for the topic, module or assignment. Each of these bibliography entries should be followed by your own brief summary and evaluation of the source.

2 Analyse your assignment title

For a given title you will often be expected to discuss the assumptions behind, tensions within and different perspectives on the relevant issue, so analyse the title carefully. Break down your title or task brief into content, instruction and scope.

C: words related to the **content** of the topic. In your assignment you will probably need to analyse and define these words.

Examples of questions for analysing a concept include:

What do you think are the core characteristics of X ?

What would you define as a borderline example of X?

Are there other concepts with which X overlaps?

F: the **instruction** or command words. Read these carefully and check you know what each one means. Note that the terms *argue* and *discuss* tend to be interpreted differently in different disciplines, so check what these involve for your assignment.

S: the **scope** – what you are asked to cover and not cover, for example specific time periods or countries. If the scope is not explicit, you will need to decide for yourself what to cover and state this clearly in your introduction.

    FROM ENGLISH LANGUAGE TEST TO UNIVERSITY SUCCESS

Below is an essay title from an MSc Civil Engineering module. The annotations show the type of questions you would need to ask yourself when analysing this title.

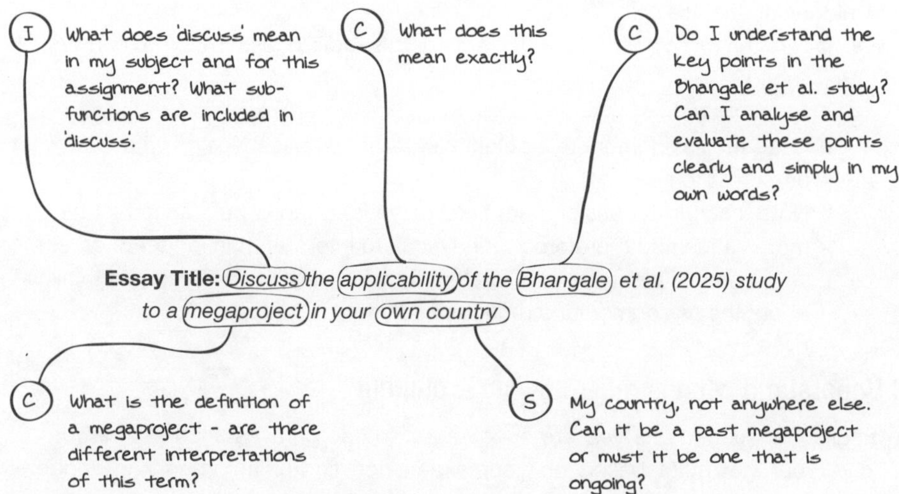

For more advice on analysing assignment titles, see *Planning Your Essay* and *Getting Critical* in this series.

Before you start planning your assignment, ask yourself:

- Why has my tutor set this assignment and what do they want to see?
- Are there any hidden issues, underlying assumptions or value judgements 'hidden' in the title?
- What are the most contentious aspects of this topic/question? What can be challenged?

- Read the assignment title objectively rather than just seeing what you want or expect to see.
- Note that shorter assignment titles may look simpler but can in fact be more vague and therefore more difficult to interpret than longer ones.
- Give yourself plenty of time (preferably a few days) to analyse and think about the assignment instructions and title.

3 Understand what is meant by 'an argument'

In English language tests you are encouraged to use phrases such as '*I argue . . .*' to give your viewpoint based on your experience and/or common knowledge. At university, however, merely giving your viewpoint is not 'arguing' and you should not use the word in this way. 'An argument' in academic study refers to a statement or claim you then support with evidence from academic research and sources. Note that 'support' in an academic argument involves using sources that both agree and disagree with your position.

To present a strong, logically developed and persuasive argument you will need to tell your reader:

why X is an important issue and worthy of discussion

what *you* are going to argue/demonstrate and why

which aspects of X are more/most important to your argument and why

what you see as lacking/problematic in the current research on X and why

what other perspectives on X exist in the field

why your perspective/conclusion/solution is the most valid.

(See also Chapter 10.)

To give you an idea of the difference between writing for an English test and for a university essay, the table below gives the first sentence/s of each paragraph for both types of writing. In the essay, the brackets indicate where source material would be used and referenced.

English language test task 250 words	University essay 1,500–2,000 words
The ways in which some advertisers market their products are unethical and can even be harmful to consumers. How far do you agree with this statement? Nowadays, advertisers sometimes use unethical methods that can . . . I believe that although this is sometimes true, advertising can also . . . One way in which adverts can hurt people is . . . Another method companies use is . . . However, beneficial effects of adverts include . . .	***What is discriminatory brand advertising (DBA) and what evidence is there that it causes stress to certain consumer groups?*** Brand marketing plays a crucial role in the economy of . . . (source references). Discriminatory advertising is defined as (source references) . . . I argue here not only that DBA causes . . . but that the degree of stress is dependent on two factors . . . The influence of both factors can be demonstrated by looking at a frequently discriminated group in this context, that of black women (source references) . . . The effect of such discriminatory marketing on this group can be seen below in Table 1. The data from (source reference) also shows that . . .

English language test task 250 words	University essay 1,500–2,000 words
To conclude, although advertising can . . . I also think that it can help people to . . .	An alternative explanation for these results is offered by (source references) who suggest that . . . Such arguments are limited, however, in that they do not include (source references) . . . The implications proposed by these studies are, I suggest, also contradicted by the fact that . . . This essay has reviewed the evidence that . . . Furthermore, we suggest that further research on . . . is needed in order to clarify . . .

4 Check whether and how you are allowed to use Gen AI

Read your course regulations on the use of AI tools and applications. These rules might, for example, state that you are allowed to use Gen AI tools to help you learn but not to help you write assignments, and so you need to understand what is meant by 'help'. If you are unclear about anything, ask your tutors. Universities generally expect you to use AI tools critically and with caution. They also expect you to be responsible and accountable for all work you produce.

Useful things to bear in mind when using Gen AI for university study are that:
- the quality of the output depends on the quality of its training data and of the prompts you input
- output can be irrelevant, non-academic, biased, out of date, vague, too simple, too complex or fabricated
- Gen AI output reflects the biases and opinions of its training data and generally presents these using a calm, neutral tone. This can lead to extreme views having the appearance of evidenced knowledge.

Useful questions to ask yourself when deciding whether to use an AI tool at university include:
- Is it worth using an AI tool for this task as I will need to check the output anyway?
- Which AI tool will be the most effective for this task?
- (How) can I use the AI tool critically?
- What are my course regulations regarding using and declaring use of generative AI tools?

ⓘ Always read the terms of use and privacy policy of any tools you use, as any work and/or personal data you upload might be stored, shared and downloaded by others, including for illegal and unethical purposes.

If you are allowed to use AI tools for an assignment, you can use them to help you analyse the title, brainstorm ideas and suggest a structure and then reflect critically on the output to develop your own ideas.

Note that universities are increasingly designing assignments that assess the process involved in producing them rather than the final product, so make sure you are clear on what you are allowed and not allowed to do *at each stage* of your assignment process.

Key points

1 Make sure you understand the task, title and marking criteria for each assignment – if anything is unclear, ask your tutor for clarification as soon as possible.
2 The point of most assignments is to develop, decide and show what *you* think.

What you need to do in an English language test	What you need to do at university
You do not have to select source material.	Search for and select source material as a fundamental part of academic work.

English language tests do not require you to choose which sources to read, listen to or watch. The test passages are usually general, factual and simplified, with the information at the level of an introductory textbook or encyclopedia. Much of the information could be considered as common knowledge. For all these reasons, knowing who wrote the passage is not seen as important and authors are not named.

At university, however, you need to both search for and select material that is specialized, with content that is often abstract, theoretical and discursive. Four points to remember are that:

▸ you should take an independent and critical approach to searching and selecting sources

- for something to count as knowledge, you need to know who created it. This is so that you can examine the context, assumptions, processes and motivations behind its creation
- there is rarely a 'perfect' source that will give you the answer to your question, and trying to find such material is not the point of doing an assignment. Nor should you be trying to find only sources that agree with you. Your tutors want you to find sources that give you a range of evidence, viewpoints and ideas
- searching for and selecting material is a key part of the academic research process.

What counts as an academic source?

Words used to describe appropriate sources are *academic*, *scholarly*, *reliable*, *authoritative*, *credible* and *rigorous*. These terms are often used interchangeably to mean that the source is written/created by someone who knows what they are talking about and whose information has been checked by other experts and deemed to be accurate, up to date and fair.

Note that what counts as suitable source material can vary according to discipline and assignment type, so check with your tutor if you are unsure. For example, you might want to purposely use 'unreliable' or non-academic material (e.g. news articles or blogs) if this is relevant for your assignment.

Non-academic source types

Text types

Textbooks

In some disciplines these are often considered as non-academic because they summarize other research, sometimes without saying where this information comes from. They also often omit the debates and contentions involved in a topic.

Newspapers

This includes quality newspapers such as *The Times* or *The Independent* and magazines such as *The Economist*, *Newsweek* and *New Scientist*.

Book or article reviews

These are not reliable sources because they are written by someone who is not the author, do not give detailed information and include the personal opinion of the reviewer.

Academic article abstracts

An article abstract is not a valid source in its own right – you need to find the information in the body of the article if you want to refer to it in an assignment.

Websites and online resources

Wikipedia articles

These can be useful for getting a basic understanding of something but are anonymous, can contain misinformation and are tertiary sources, bringing together information from many different sources.

YouTube videos, TED talks and blogs

These can be used as source material if the speaker is authoritative and references information.

Websites ending with .com or .org

Note that government publications can be used as source material if the authors/organizations are known, are authoritative and reference the information they contain.

Websites that have marketing or journalistic content

These sites often contain words such as *magazine*, *digest*, *personals*, *news*, *press release*, *correspondent*, *journalist*, *special report*, *classified* and *advert*.

Search engines

These are not sources. Do not list them as references in your assignments.

Gen AI output

AI output is not produced by a person or an organization. It is a product of the various reliable and unreliable sources in its training data. Do not list AI tools as academic references in your assignments.

Below is a list of sources on the topic of ethical marketing, with a comment on whether they would count as academic sources.

Source search for 'Is there such a thing as ethical marketing?'	Source type	Is it an academic source?
https://wisepops.com/blog/ethical-marketing	Someone's blog.	no
https://www.bbpress.co.uk/news/ethical-marketing-examples-of-brands-who-have-got-it-spot-on	A news piece.	no
Kamila, M. K., Jasrotia, S. S. and Chib, S. (2024). Digital enigma: Understanding ethical dilemmas in design and marketing. In *Review of Technologies and Disruptive Business Strategies*, 67–82. Emerald Publishing.	A paper in a recent issue of a journal.	yes

Source search for 'Is there such a thing as ethical marketing?'	Source type	Is it an academic source?
https://en.wikipedia.org/wiki/Ethical_marketing	A Wikipedia entry.	no
https://www.ivoryresearch.com/samples/essay-on-ethics-and-marketing/	A site where you can buy essays.	no
Laczniak, G. R. and Murphy, P. E. (1991). Fostering ethical marketing decisions. *Journal of Business Ethics*, *10*, 259–71.	A paper in an old issue of a journal.	yes (but it is not recent)
Article abstract for: Durif, F., Graf, R., Chaput, M. A., Ducharme, R. and Elbakkali, A. (2009). Do ethics have a place in marketing? An overview of the last 20 years. *Innovative Marketing*, *5*(1).	The abstract of a journal article.	no
https://www.goodreads.com/book/show/1038094.Ethical_Marketing	A book review on a bookseller's website.	no

So, what can you do to bridge the gap?

1 Take control of your reading list

Take control of your course or module reading list. Your tutors do not want you to read everything on the list – they want to see that you can select relevant material. Note that even within the 'required', 'essential' or 'core' sections of your reading list there will probably be several titles that cover similar ground.

Reflecting briefly on *all* the titles on your reading list (including those you decide not to read) will help you become familiar with the authors in your field.

2 Have a starting purpose and position

Reflect on your current views and questions on the issue. Using this starting position, decide on your purpose and focus for your source search and selection. Your purpose might be broad at first (for example, to learn about a new topic), but you do need some kind of starting point, otherwise you will waste a lot of time with searches that are too general or vague.

3 Be specific

Don't search using just the main topic, e.g. 'exoplanets'. Instead, use your specific issue or question as the search input. For example, 'How does the composition of exoplanets affect their habitability?'. If you are using a Boolean search technique, you would enter 'exoplanets AND composition AND habitability'.

4 Use subject-specific gateways and databases

General search engines such as Google Scholar can be useful (particularly if you already know the title or author) but their databases are not comprehensive, fully up-to-date or checked for academic credibility. Instead, use the subject gateways recommended by your tutors such as JSTOR, ScienceDirect or Scopus.

5 Know the *who*, *what* and *why* of each source you select

Source checklist	✓
What type of source is it?	
Who wrote it, when and why?	
Who has it been written for?	
Is it academic and, if not, is that okay for why you want to use it?	
Why are you going to read it – what exactly do you want to get out of it?	
Do you think it will support your conclusion or give a different viewpoint?	

Check the academic credibility of the journals you use – some websites titled 'academic' or 'journal' are in fact not reliable. Check whether the journal has a peer-review process and read the 'about us' and 'editorial process' tabs on its website, and/or look at its Wikipedia entry.

The number of sources you use in an assignment should match the importance and/or scale of the point you are using them for – you will probably need to use more sources to support major points than you will for more minor ones.

6 Own your source selection

Building up your own selection of relevant sources is hard work and is a key part of academic research. Keep a record of the full bibliographic details of each source and note down when and where you found each one. You should discuss and share individual sources with other students (doing this an important part of academic study) but avoid sharing the whole list of sources you have found and selected yourself – this detective work is what will help make your assignment unique and it belongs to you.

Key points

1 Decide on your initial position and questions before you start searching for and selecting sources.
2 Select sources that are as specific as possible to your assignment.
3 It is *your* responsibility to check the authorship and credibility of all your source material.
4 The source selection you create is unique and an essential part of producing an original assignment; it therefore belongs to you.

For more advice, see *Where's Your Evidence?* in this series.

What you need to do in an English language test	What you need to do at university
Answer short comprehension questions or describe the content of short texts on general and/or familiar topics, e.g. electoral systems. The texts are often simplified extracts from textbooks, magazines and newspapers and usually have a semi-formal, journalistic style. Skim and scan texts and read some texts/text sections in detail. You are allowed to make notes but these are not usually part of the test.	Analyse and evaluate subject-specific, often quite long, complex texts. You will often have a high reading load. Common text types are academic articles and books, reports and case studies. Most texts have a formal structure and style. Skim and/or scan to select texts or text sections and then read these in detail using a critical approach. Make notes according to your reading purpose. Effective note-making is important for academic work, and notes are sometimes required as part of an assignment submission.

Reading

English language test passages

These tend to be factual and neutral, giving information and sometimes different views, but without a clear author perspective and, indeed, the authors are not named. In terms of style, most ELT reading passages are slightly informal and/or journalistic. The example test extract below illustrates these aspects of English language test passages.

Extract 1

Design in education: The classroom chair

By and large, classroom chairs have traditionally been made out of durable and non-expensive materials, with designs based on practicality rather than student comfort, learning or safety. Since then though, there have been many developments in classroom chair design, and nowadays chairs can include features such as adjustable seats and wheelchair integration. It is clear that school chair designs should also take the learning environment into account; most modern classroom chairs can, for example, be easily moved and grouped in different ways.

English language test visual data

In most tests you also need to read some simple visual data. No author, context or author viewpoint is given with the data. An example of this type of visual data text is given below.

Extract 2

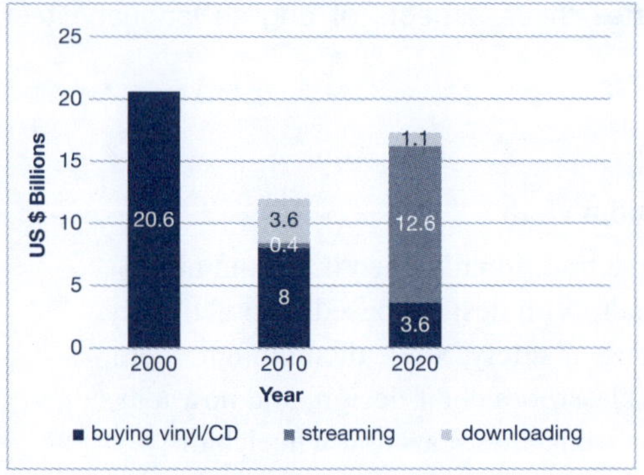

Revenue sources in the global music industry

English language test tasks

These assess your understanding of the content of both written and visual data texts. You are usually asked comprehension questions and/or to describe what the text says or shows. In other words, you are asked to say what is *inside* the text.

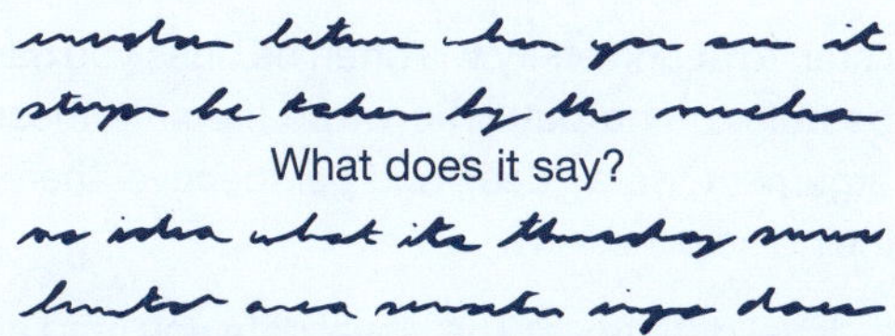

What does it say?

Example question for Extract 1:

Select the best answer. Classroom chairs used to be:

A) practical more than comfortable.

B) cheap but easily breakable.

C) designed to encourage learning.

Example task for Extract 2:

Summarize the information given in the chart, describing the main trends and making comparisons where relevant.

University texts

The texts you read, watch and listen to at university will often be ones you have chosen, and you will always know (or be able to find out) who wrote them. In these texts the authors will present their own argument, data, ideas and perspective, thereby making a 'knowledge contribution' to their discipline.

This applies to both written and visual data texts. The visual data you read at university might be simple (as in Extract 2) or it might be complex, but you will usually know who the author is and how and why they are using the data.

As examples, below are extracts from two academic texts in which the authors contribute to their field by presenting an informed viewpoint.

Extract 3

The modern classroom chair: Exploring the 'coercive design' of contemporary schooling

. . . it [is] notable that the three chair designs featured in this paper [are] . . . deeply conservative products – promising to not disrupt the fundamental order of the classroom and to reinforce the basic idea of students staying in their seats and working. Thus, as Fuller (2019) continues, 'much of what [designers] call "creative" today is not creative at all but rather cementing the status quo, forever in the service of capital, labour, and consumption'.

Extract from: Selwyn, N. (2024). The modern classroom chair: Exploring the 'coercive design' of contemporary schooling. *Power and Education*, *16*(1), 63–77, p. 74.

Extract 4
Revolutionizing drug delivery systems: Nanotechnology-based approaches for targeted therapy

As we advance, the potential for nanotechnology to revolutionize drug delivery systems remains immense. The ongoing development and refinement of nanotechnology-based approaches offer hope for more effective, personalized treatments that can improve patient outcomes and address some of the most challenging medical conditions. With continued research and collaboration, nanotechnology has the power to reshape the landscape of targeted therapy and pave the way for a new era in precision medicine.

Extract from: Emeihe, E. V., Nwankwo, E. I., Ajegbile, M. D., Olaboye, J. A. and Maha, C. C. (2024). Revolutionizing drug delivery systems: Nanotechnology-based approaches for targeted therapy. *International Journal of Life Science Research Archive*, 7(1), 40–58, p. 50.

University reading

At university, rather than just describing what is inside a text you also need to look at what is behind it and what is between it and other texts. Reflecting on all these three aspects of a text will enable you to analyse, evaluate and use it to help develop your own ideas. You should take this approach for all types of texts, including visual data.

Reading texts for university study

Reading purpose: Why have I decided to read/listen to/watch/look at this text?

Looking behind the text: Who has written it? Who for? Why have they written it?

Looking inside the text:

What does the author say?
What do they try to do?

Analysis:
Valid data?
Logical argument?
Logical conclusion?
What does it *not* say?

Looking between texts:

How does it connect to other texts on the topic?

Which other authors does it support or disagree with?

Evaluation: Do I think the text is credible/important/minor/contentious/derivative? Why?
To what extent do I agree/disagree with the author? Why?
(Has) how has the author's ideas helped develop my own?

Examples of the differences between English language test and university reading

The table below uses Extract 3 on p. 61 to show you what the differences between understanding a text for an ELT test and for university study look like (although you would not be given an academic article in an English test).

Expected understanding for an English language test	Example understanding and thoughts for university study
The three classroom chairs discussed are designed to encourage students to sit down and work. In this respect, these chairs are not good examples of what we think of when we talk of creative design. Designers are not being creative but are being conservative and are helping to keep power structures in place and maintain the status quo.	Selwyn (2024) uses the example of school chairs and cites Fuller (2019) to support his main argument that designers, rather than being truly creative, often just follow normative designs and in doing so perpetuate a status quo in which students are powerless – this is what he means by 'coercive design'. I think Selwyn's conclusion is not very clear. Is he calling for designers to be more radical? To be more active in trying to use their designs to change the status quo? Selwyn also makes generalizations and does not present other points of view and other ways school chairs are designed and used. Perhaps this is because Selwyn's research position is that schools are used to control children in various ways – see e.g. Andrejevic and Selwyn (2020) . . .

Here is another example, this time using the visual data given in Extract 2 on p. 58.

Required understanding for an English language test	Expected understanding and thoughts for university study
The chart shows the different sources of income for the music industry globally in three different years – 2000, 2010 and 2020. From the data we can see that in 2000 the music industry received all its income from physical sales of records and CDs. By 2010 there had been two significant changes. One was that total income had dropped from just over 20 billion US dollars to about 12 billion, and the second that downloading was now an important part of the industry's revenue . . .	The chart is a simplified set from more detailed data published in the International Federation of the Phonographic Industry (ifpi) Global Music Report 2025, p. 4. The most interesting piece of data in this chart for me is the huge increase in income from streaming – from only a fraction of total industry music revenue in 2010 to nearly three quarters in 2020. This data supports that of . . . and shows why it is important that the industry tackles the issue of artists' music rights and payments – this is what I plan to write about in my report. What the data does not show is the factors behind this increase and the impact it is having/will have on individual musician earnings, so I need to find data on this. I also need to read the whole ifpi report and look at the more detailed data given there to see if it addresses my ideas and to check the report for music industry bias . . .

# So, what can you do to bridge the gap?

Be aware of the aspects we have looked at in this chapter and keep in mind that at university *you* usually have to decide:

> what to read

> why you have decided to read a text

> what questions to ask yourself about it.

. . . and that when you read a text you need to look at what is inside, behind and between texts.

Tips for understanding written texts

1 Academic articles have abstracts in which the authors summarize their paper. The reporting verbs (e.g. *explaining, analysing, arguing, disagreeing*) they use in their abstract will help you understand the different things they are trying to do in their article. As an example, here is the first part of the abstract from the Selwyn (2024) paper with the reporting verbs given in bold.

Abstract

This paper **explores** the role of material design as a form of institutional power within contemporary school settings. **Drawing on** concepts of 'coercive design' and 'hostile architecture' from design studies, the paper **examines** three 'innovative' designs for classroom chairs – relatively mundane but integral elements of the regulation and disciplining of school space. It is **argued** that the design . . .

2 To help deal with a high reading load, make decisions about which sources you only need to read quickly and/or partially and which texts/text sections you need to read in more detail. Start with easier texts and build up to the more difficult ones.

3 For the texts you want to read in detail, read the title, subtitles and abstract and make sure you understand these properly. Then go back and read the first and last paragraph of the text. Then go back again and read the first sentence of each paragraph, again, making sure you understand them. Finally, go back and read the whole text.

4 Read the text and summarize it in your own words. Then upload the source to a Gen AI application and ask it to summarize the main points, simplify definitions and give the key terms. Read the AI output critically and compare it with your own summary.

5 Upload the text to a Gen AI application and prompt it to help you think critically and deeply about the text; even the process of creating clear AI prompts will help develop your thought processes. Check and reflect on the AI output and then use it to create further prompts.

Example prompts:

I am a first-year undergraduate student studying X. Ask me thought-provoking questions about/questions about the methodology/the data used in this article.

I am a student studying X and I am a non-expert/an expert in this subject. Read this article and ask me easy/difficult questions about the statements/arguments made in the text.

Making notes

The point of making notes on your reading is to help you understand and reflect critically on the text. You can also use the note-making process to start re-expressing the author's information and ideas in your own way, using your own words and style.

Make notes in any way that is useful to you, including using your main language (or a combination of your main language and English), highlighting and annotating the text and using online note-making tools.

Checklist for effective notes ✓

Do your notes:
- include full bibliographic details of the text and the date the notes were created
- include a key to abbreviations you have used
- record clearly which words/phrases you have copied from the text, which you have changed only slightly (close paraphrase) and which are your own
- record clearly which are the author's ideas and comments and which are your own
- comment on how/whether the text addresses your initial reading reasons and questions
- comment on your questions and thoughts on the text and ideas for further reading/research?

As a brief example, below is the first part of some student notes on the Selwyn (2024) article.

Selwyn, N. (2024). The modern classroom chair: Exploring the 'coercive design' of contemporary schooling. *Power and Education*, 16(1), 63–77, p. 74. (I found this article via JSTOR, accessed February 2026.) CP = close paraphrase. QT = quotation. S = Selwyn. sch = school. sts = students.	My pre-reading Qs: *What does S mean by 'coercive design'?* *Does the designer consciously design something that is coercive or does it depend on who uses it and how?*
Content notes Intro and 1st section pp. 63–65 (and throughout) S argues that schools are overtly about learning but in fact are really about controlling students. QT p. 64 – 'In a basic sense, then, school is an institution characterized by a set of practices, arrangements and techniques aimed at governing students in a continuous and regulated fashion.' CP p. 74 – sch chair designs support idea sts should stay in their seats and work. . . .	**My comments, questions, thoughts** This is the main premise and paradigm of S's whole argument. But Selwyn never questions this premise or presents other views. Just Western schools? What other views are there re. what a sch is for? I need to see if there are other sources that refute S's premise. . . .

Reading and reflecting on your notes and then *using* them in some way will activate them in your mind and help you develop your own ideas. You can use your notes to summarize in your own words the main point of each paragraph of the text and/or of the whole text. You can also try re-expressing your notes in a different format (for example changing linear written notes into a spidergram) to see what new connections this creates in your mind.

Key points

1 English language tasks ask you to describe *what* is in texts, whereas university reading is about the *why.*
2 Nearly all university students find the high reading load challenging but you are not supposed to read everything – search and select sources according to your purpose.
3 Difficult academic texts will become easier to understand as you develop your subject knowledge.
4 Making, reflecting on and using your notes will help you develop your ideas and your ability to express them.

For more advice, see *Reading and Making Notes* in this series.

What you need to do in an English language test	What you need to do at university
The ability to develop your own ideas and position is not tested. Most writing tasks ask you to relate the topic points to your personal experience and/or opinion.	Develop your own informed ideas and position on subject-specific issues. It is not usually acceptable to use personal experience and/or opinion that is not supported by evidence from academic sources.

What do university tutors mean by 'originality'?

The conclusions you reach in your academic assignments should be yours, and university assessment marking criteria contain words such as *original*, *unique*, *innovative*, *creative* and *insightful* to describe this idea of developing your own, informed position.

This does *not* mean that university tutors expect you to come up with a whole new idea, theory or data set. What they want is for you to develop your own informed ideas and position on topics and issues in your field. What tutors look for is how well students have used, reflected on and compared different sources in their own way, to reach their own insight, solution or conclusion.

 ## So, what can you do to bridge the gap?

Reflect, question, connect

Take a reflective approach to all aspects of your study – both focussed, purposeful reflection on what you learn and the more relaxed, background thinking you do when you are doing something else. Focussed reflection should include both criticality (analysing, questioning, evaluating) and connecting knowledge by taking a step back to 'join the dots' between different ideas, evidence and perspectives.

Allow yourself to connect ideas between all your areas of study, including across modules and levels.

It doesn't matter if these connections don't make sense at first – sometimes the best and most original ideas come from unconscious and unplanned thought processes.

FROM ENGLISH LANGUAGE TEST TO UNIVERSITY SUCCESS

By reflecting, questioning and connecting, you are, in fact, producing your own original 'pattern' or way of seeing. Your perspective will, to a greater or lesser extent, be different from that of other students doing the same assignment. Even if everyone reads the same sources, your conclusion is likely to be unique because of how *you* have interpreted the assignment title, the position *you* have started from, which sections of the sources *you* have used and how *you* have connected them.

Even if your conclusion is similar to that of other students, your assignment will still be original because of the aspects you have emphasized, the sources you have used and the questions you have asked in order to reach it. You can also enhance the uniqueness of your assignment by 'going that bit further', suggesting additional questions, tensions and areas of future research.

As you progress in your studies, you will have the opportunity to be even more original by, for example, creating your own research questions, using a novel technique or methodology for gathering data, applying a standard technique to novel material, and/ or refining or extending what other researchers have done.

Originality is a process not a product

Doing the things we have covered so far will help you develop your own ideas:

- think critically, reflectively, independently and creatively (See Chapter 2.)

- understand the point and purpose of your course assignments (See Chapter 5.)
- reflect on what you think about the assignment issue/question and use this starting position to decide how you will approach it and therefore what information and sources you will search for and select (See Chapter 6.)
- understand, critically analyse and evaluate what your source authors say by looking inside, behind and between texts (See Chapter 7.)
- join up the dots and reflect on why you have joined them in this way. (This chapter.)

You can also input prompts into a Gen AI tool to help you brainstorm ideas and to generate further questions on which to reflect.

What should you do if you have an idea and then find the same one in a source text?

It is common to have a view or idea and then come across a similar one in a published source. Note down your idea (and importantly, *why* you think it is good) so that you keep it clearly in your mind. Then as you read, make a careful note of which sources have the same or a similar idea to yours. As you continue reading, you will probably find that your idea and reasons for it are (slightly) different from those of the source authors. Whether it is or not, in your assignment you can propose your idea first and use the source authors' idea as support for yours, discussing the ways in which they are, similar and different. The key thing is to acknowledge (reference) the author in your work and make them part of your 'story', rather than pretend they don't exist.

Key points

1 Reflect, question and connect.
2 Don't be afraid to risk being wrong by presenting your own idea – just make sure you give logical reasoning and/or evidence to support it.
3 Originality does not depend on level of intelligence but on thinking critically.

For more on developing ideas and critical thinking, see *Where's Your Argument?* in this series.

What you need to do in an English language test	What you need to do at university
Produce a short summary and/or paraphrase of fairly simple texts, and/or describe simple visual data.	Use a range of source material in a critical way. Analyse and evaluate sources you have selected. Use them in your work by grouping/summarizing/paraphrasing/quoting in ways that emphasize your points and support your own argument. (Note that 'support' means using sources that both disagree and agree with your perspective.)
Full and clear source acknowledgement is not tested. Partial or absence of source acknowledgement is acceptable.	Fully acknowledge all sources, using different referencing techniques to emphasize different aspects of the material.
The ability to show clear differentiation between your ideas and sources is not tested.	Use referencing techniques to make clear which ideas are yours and which are those of source authors.

English language tests

The texts you are required to read and then use in speaking or writing tasks are either anonymous or give only vague or partial information about sources, for example, *'experiments have shown'*, *'research by Dr Xu'*. The tasks do not require you to always distinguish clearly between your ideas and those of the source texts.

University-level work

For academic study, you need to know who has produced any material you use in order to assess its credibility and value. Moreover, you must state explicitly where this information has come from (referred to as citing, referencing or acknowledging). You need to acknowledge source material because:

- you need to give credit to the person/organization that produced the piece of knowledge; this is part of the good scholarship practice that your tutors will expect of you
- you need to show your tutor what current knowledge you have used and how you have used it to build new knowledge.

The extracts below show you the difference between how you use source material in an ELT writing task and in a university assignment.

English language test writing task (Extracts from a suggested answer)	First-year student report (Extract from the introduction)
Is urban farming beneficial to the environment? This report will look at urban farming data and then outline the advantages and disadvantages of this type of farming. According to recent statistics, last year the global urban farming market was worth about five and a half billion dollars and is predicted to be worth nearly 14 billion by 2030.	**A SWOT analysis of vertical and hydroponic farming in Rosario, Argentina** The number of vertical and hydroponic farms have increased over the past decade. Growing at a rate of nearly 9% annually and with a current global value of approximately 174 billion US dollars, urban farming represents a large and viable market (Urban Farming Global Market Report 2025, p. 1).

No sources acknowledged

Specific source

Advantages of urban farming.

Farmers can use urban farming techniques to control the growing environment, such as soil quality, amount of water used, temperature and the amount of light the crops get . . .

Disadvantages.

However, urban farming can be very expensive to set up and needs specialized equipment and expertise. It also uses a great deal of energy and water, and according to some

In Argentina, urban farming is also emerging as an exciting new market, particularly in cities such as Rosario (the largest city in Santa Fe province). Here, a vertical, hydroponic farm was established in 2002 which now covers 185 acres of the city (Hammelman et al. 2022).

Research conducted by Lawson and Taylor (2020) shows the potential for the urban farming market but also the challenges faced by this sector that arise from its complex environmental and business context. This current report examines the potential environmental

groups, is therefore not sustainable in the long term. In addition, urban farms can only grow a small number of food varieties . . .

for the continued growth of the market for urban farming in Rosario, using a SWOT analysis (strengths, weaknesses, opportunities and threats) of both the internal and external market factors . . .

References:
Hammelman, C., Shoffner, E., Cruzat, M. and Lee, S., 2022. Assembling agroecological socio-natures: A political ecology analysis of urban and peri-urban agriculture in Rosario, Argentina. *Agriculture and Human Values*, 39(1), 371–83.

. . .

FROM ENGLISH LANGUAGE TEST TO UNIVERSITY SUCCESS

Referencing styles

Different academic disciplines use different referencing styles (for example, Harvard, APA, Chicago) and your course tutors will advise you on this. Whichever style you use you must always do two things – give a reference next to where you have used the source in your writing (author and year or a number) AND give the full details of each source at the end of your assignment, referred to as list of references or bibliography.

In-text citations

In your writing you can either:

1 Use the authors as the subject of a sentence, for example:

Lawson and Taylor (2020) have shown that . . .

Research conducted by Lawson and Taylor (2020) shows that . . .

or

For more on referencing styles, see *Referencing, Understanding Plagiarism and Ethical AI* in this series.

2 Give the citation at the end of the sentence, for example:

Research has shown the potential for the urban farming market but also the challenges arising from its particular business and environmental context (Lawson and Taylor 2020).

The Chinese fashion industry needs to do much more to meet the United Nation's Sustainable Development Goals [3].

You can use both techniques in the same piece of writing – the 'author as subject' technique to emphasize who wrote something and the 'information first' technique to emphasize the idea or piece of information.

Summarizing, paraphrasing and quoting

Summarizing

This is the most common method of using source material in academic writing. You can often use just one sentence or phrase to summarize an author's main point or even the position of several authors who hold a similar view.

For example:

> *A SWOT analysis is often used to examine an organization's external and internal environment as an early-stage strategy and decision-making tool (Helms and Nixon 2010; Gurl 2017; Paul and Cadle 2020).*

Summarizing source material allows you to:
- show that you understand the source/s
- show that you can group several sources under one main idea or position
- re-express the source/s in a way that supports your argument
- re-express the source/s clearly and simply, using your own words and writing style
- integrate the source/s smoothly into your assignment.

When you summarize you must:
- use mostly (roughly 90%) your own words, style and sentence pattern
- acknowledge the source in your writing AND in the list of references at the end of your assignment.

Paraphrasing

This is when you re-express a specific piece of information, point or idea from a source.

For example:

Original source extract:

> *. . .The urban farming market size has grown strongly in recent years. It will grow from $159.92 billion in 2024 to $174.23 billion in 2025 at a compound annual growth rate (CAGR) of 8.9% . . .*
>
> Extract from: Urban Farming Global Market Report 2025, p. 1.

Student paraphrase:

> *Urban farming is growing at a rate of nearly 9% annually and has a current global value of approximately 174 billion US dollars (Urban Farming Global Market Report 2025, p. 1).*

Paraphrasing source material allows you to:

- show your tutor that you understand the source
- select the information and ideas that support your argument

 FROM ENGLISH LANGUAGE TEST TO UNIVERSITY SUCCESS

- re-express the source in a way that supports your argument
- re-express the source clearly and simply, using your own words and writing style
- integrate the source into your assignment.

When you paraphrase you must:
- use mostly (roughly 90%) of your own words, style and sentence pattern
- acknowledge the source in your writing AND in the list of references at the end of your assignment.

Quoting

Quoting from source material is more common in the arts and humanities than in the sciences – your course tutors will give you guidance on whether you should use quotations or not.

Why quote?
- To give a definition.
- To convey a fact or idea that the author has expressed in a powerful, unique, useful or interesting way.

① Do not use too many quotations in an assignment – tutors usually prefer you to show that you have understood the source and can integrate it into your work by using summary and paraphrase.

When you quote you must:

- use quotation marks for short quotations and indentation for longer ones
- not make any changes to the original text (If you need to make any changes, use ellipses to delete something or [ ] to add something that is not in the original text.)

For example:

'Nanotechnology has the power to reshape the landscape of targeted therapy . . .' (Emeihe et al. 2024, p. 50).

- acknowledge the source in your writing AND in your list of references at the end of the assignment.

 ## So, what can you do to bridge the gap?

1 Make sure you understand the source

Don't use material in your work unless you understand it fully and accurately – you should be able to re-express and summarize what the author says simply and clearly in your own words, as if you are explaining the source to a friend. If you then summarize or paraphrase the source in your work, keep it simple, again using your own words in a simple and clear style. If you use Gen AI tools to create a source summary, try writing your own first and then critically compare the two versions.

2 Be clear on your reason for using it

Think about *why* you want to use the source. Is it to give a definition? To give some background information? To summarize relevant research? To give a powerful statement from a major source? To show the range of views on an issue? To provide evidence for a claim you are making?

Check that the source you use demonstrates your point *exactly*, rather than just being vaguely about the same topic. Being clear on why you want to use a source will help you decide the best way to integrate it into your assignment – summary, paraphrase or quotation.

3 Don't just describe – analyse and evaluate

A common reason for low marks in assignments is that they are too 'descriptive' – the student has just described what sources say. You should use your source critically, perhaps briefly summarizing what they say but then going on to analyse and evaluate them in support of your argument.

Description – gives the 'what' but does not analyse, explain or evaluate and does not try to persuade. Description can include explanation (e.g. *this is because/the reason for this is*) but it is still descriptive if it merely restates the explanation given in the source.

Example of descriptive writing:

Zhang et al. (2024) show that the dimensions currently used to measure well-being give valid data for these parameters. They point out that the reason for this is that . . .

Analysis – breaking something down into its separate parts and examining and defining each part in detail. You will often need to do this when discussing concepts, ideas and data.

Example of analytical writing:

Zhang et al. (2024) define well-being as . . . In this definition well-being is perceived by the individual and is therefore a subjective measure. The authors include the cognitive aspects of life from a holistic perspective but not aspects such as . . . This definition differs from that of . . .

Evaluation – using what you have learnt from your analysis to evaluate the strengths and weaknesses of the whole argument and idea, giving an informed judgement of its validity, credibility, value, implications and impact.

Example of evaluative writing:

The Zhang et al. review suggests that the well-being dimensions and the measurement scales in which they are used do have a high level of internal

     FROM ENGLISH LANGUAGE TEST TO UNIVERSITY SUCCESS

consistency, validity and reliability. However, internal validity does not equate to external reliability, and we have argued here that the focus of the scale is, on the one hand too narrow . . . and yet also defines 'satisfaction' too broadly . . . This is likely to limit the scale's ability to measure all aspects of well-being . . .

4 Use language to show your position in relation to the source

Use adjectives, verbs and phrases that reflect your position. If you are going to agree with a source you can use either positive verbs (e.g. *show, demonstrate, establish, confirm*) or neutral/open ones (*suggest, state, maintain, claim*). If you are going to disagree with the source, use only neutral/open verbs. For example:

Agreeing with a source:

*Zhang et al. (2024) have conducted a **comprehensive** review that **shows** that valid data on well-being can be collected by using the four established dimensions currently used by researchers. Evidence that these current measures **are indeed effective** can be seen . . .*

For more advice, see *Getting Critical* in this series.

*Zhang et al. (2024) **suggest** that valid data on well-being can be collected by using the four established dimensions currently used by researchers. Evidence that these current measures are **indeed effective** can be seen . . .*

Disagreeing with a source:

*Zhang et al. (2024) **suggest** that valid data on well-being can be collected by using the four established categories currently used by researchers. **However, this perspective is biased** in that it only considers . . .*

5 Make sure your reader knows why you are using a source

Always give your own point or comment before and/or after any source summary, paraphrase or quotation. Your reader wants to know exactly why you have put it in your assignment.

For example:

6 Make every switch between you and your sources clear

Your tutor needs to know which ideas are yours and which aren't, so use in-text citations and 'citation reminder phrases' to show each switch between your points and those of source authors. A rule of academic writing is that if a sentence does not mention a source in any way, it is assumed to be the writer's (your) own idea.

In the following example, the student has used citations – or not – to correctly show which ideas are theirs and which are from sources. Comments on how they have done this are given on the right.

The four dimensions normally used to collect well-being data are too restrictive and non-inclusive. A recent review of well-being studies shows that in order to measure overall well-being effectively, the distinctions between the categories need to be clarified and that further categories should be added (Zhang et al. 2024). The authors also demonstrate that well-being studies have excluded non-Western populations, and that this needs to be remedied if valid data of overall well-being is to be collected. Three key dimensions that need to be included in future studies are, I would suggest, . . .	1st sentence – the student does not give a citation, which shows the tutor that this is their own idea. 2nd sentence – the student introduces the source and gives a citation at the end, showing the tutor that this idea comes from a source. 3rd sentence – the student used the phrase 'The authors also', reminding the tutor that this sentence is a continuation of the source paraphrase. 4th sentence – the student does not give a citation, showing the tutor that this is their own point.

Key points

1 Being able to use source material correctly and effectively starts with good scholarship practices such as selecting, reading and making notes on source material purposely and critically.

2 Be clear in your own mind exactly *why* you are using each source – if you're not sure, don't use it.

3 Don't just describe – analyse and evaluate.

4 Make all the switches between 'you' and 'source' clear to your reader.

5 You are responsible for everything in your assignment – it is your name on the front page.

What you need to do in an English language test	What you need to do at university
Communicate information and views on a familiar topic.	Communicate a developed academic argument using integrated source material. Convey ideas clearly and precisely using formal but non-complex language.
Use a semi-formal and/or journalistic writing style.	Use an academic, disciplinary style.
Demonstrate use of language functions (e.g. comparing, agreeing), linking words, signposting language and a range of grammatical structures and vocabulary.	The use and range of language, grammar, vocabulary, linking words and signposting language are not tested.
Phrases such as *I think/I believe/In my opinion/In my experience we should/must* are acceptable.	Phrases such as *I think/I believe/In my opinion/In my experience we should/must* are not usually acceptable.

English language test written tasks

These assess your ability to describe information and to then present your own viewpoint. The test examiners mark both for content and for language proficiency, including range of grammatical forms and vocabulary.

University-level written assignments

For academic study, communicating good-quality content in a clear way is more important than demonstrating you can use a range of linguistic features used to do so. In other words, academic tutors are not testing you on how many different words you know, whether you can construct complex sentences or whether you have perfect grammar. What tutors want to see is complex, evidence-based ideas expressed in clear, precise language.

 ## So, what can you do to bridge the gap?

1 Remember the points covered in Chapters 1–9:

- understand the ways of thinking and valued skills of your discipline
- understand your assignment title and why your tutor has set it
- have your own starting position on the assignment question

- use your starting position to search for and select relevant reading
- look inside, behind and between texts to reflect on, question and connect different perspectives
- connect and contrast source perspectives with your own developed and informed position
- demonstrate critical understanding and use of sources, making clear to your reader which ideas are yours.

2 Support your statements with evidence

For example, each statement below would need to be supported by evidence from sources.

Urban farming is expensive.

Pollution is a growing problem.

Brand advertising is crucial to retail companies.

Western societies tend to have high levels of consumerism.

  FROM ENGLISH LANGUAGE TEST TO UNIVERSITY SUCCESS

The only types of statements you should make without evidence are those that convey specific, undebatable facts. For example:

Samia Suluhu Hassan became president of the United Republic of Tanzania in March 2021.

Santiago is the capital of Chile.

There are 12 Chinese zodiac signs.

3 Structure your argument using logical order of content

In Chapter 5 we looked at the essay skeleton below. Here are parts of it again, this time with comments on what the student does in each paragraph to show you how their essay is structured.

Essay title: *What is discriminatory brand advertising (DBA) and what evidence is there that it causes stress to certain consumer groups?*

What the student is doing in each paragraph	First sentence(s) of each paragraph
Gives the context and definitions and states what they are going to argue.	Brand marketing plays a crucial role in . . . (source references). I argue here not only that DBA causes . . . but that . . .
Provides support for their point.	The influence of both factors can be demonstrated by looking at a frequently discriminated group in this context, that of black women (source references) . . .
Provides further support for their point.	The effect of such discriminatory marketing on this group can be seen below in . . .
Presents counter-arguments.	An alternative explanation for these results is offered by (source references) who suggest that . . .
Challenges these counter-arguments.	Such arguments are limited, however, in that they do not include (references) . . . The implications proposed by these studies are, I suggest, also contradicted by the fact that . . .
Concludes and takes things further.	This essay has reviewed the evidence that . . . Furthermore, we suggest that further research is needed in order to clarify . . .

 FROM ENGLISH LANGUAGE TEST TO UNIVERSITY SUCCESS

A note on signposting language

Notice that in the essay skeleton above only one linking word (*however*) is used to structure and connect the essay paragraphs. At university, you will need to use some linking words and other signposting language, but you are not being tested on your ability to do so. Using lots of signposting language will not make your writing 'academic' and will not compensate for weak content.

Using Gen AI to help you structure your assignment

You can prompt an AI tool to put your assignment points into a key word or bullet structure, or to create an outline. You can then critique the AI output to brainstorm and develop further your own ideas for both content and structure. Note that you will probably need to declare that you have used an AI tool in this way as part of your assignment process.

4 Develop a clear and precise writing style

Use sentence structures that help your reader

Some of the texts you read at university might use long, complicated sentences, but these are not good examples to follow. Your tutors want you to write using clear and relatively simple language and structures. As a guideline, don't have lots of sentences that have more than three parts (referred to as clauses).

The sentence below has three clauses (separated by /).

Research conducted by Lawson and Taylor (2020) shows the potential for urban farming markets/but also the challenges of this sector/that arise from its complex environmental context.

Use nouns

Most academic writing discusses ideas and information rather than individuals doing things. It also needs to be concise and to focus the reader's attention on the main ideas. These aspects are reflected in the fact that academic writing tends to use noun phrases more than subject + verb phrases.

FROM ENGLISH LANGUAGE TEST TO UNIVERSITY SUCCESS

For example:

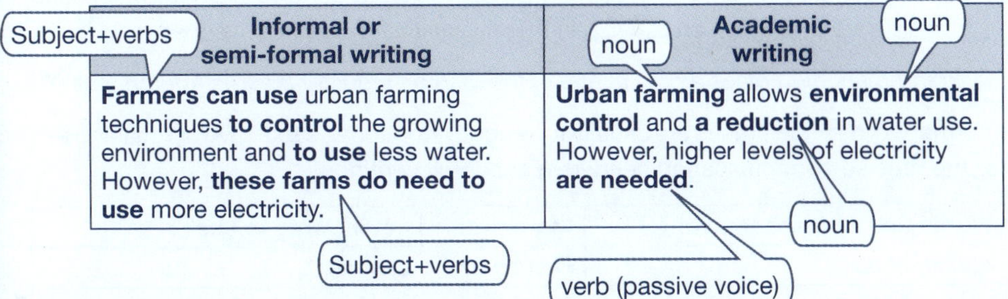

Use words to communicate clearly

Use formal words because they are precise, not because you think they make your work look 'academic'. In fact, tutors would rather you use simple language and repeat words to express your ideas precisely, rather than use complicated vocabulary that makes your meaning less clear.

For example:

This essay will commence by establishing that the literature shows that brand marketing plays a paramount and crucial role in the fashion industry (source references). 

Brand marketing plays a crucial role in the fashion industry (source references). ✓

Informal words and phrases are usually too vague, emotional, subjective or meaningless for the precise communication needed in academic writing.

Words and phrases to avoid	More precise equivalents to use
At first, at last,	*First/firstly Last/lastly*
In the end/At the end	*To summarize/In summary To conclude/In conclusion*
Basically,	*Basically* is a redundant word – just start the sentence without it.
Like	*Such as, For example*
etc./and so on/and so forth	*such as X, Y and Z/ for example X, Y and Z*
And besides/Besides/Besides this	*In addition/Moreover/As well as X there is/ There is also*
Next I will discuss/Then there is	*Another/A second /A different/A more important*

FROM ENGLISH LANGUAGE TEST TO UNIVERSITY SUCCESS

Thing/stuff	Use the specific noun, e.g. *problem/material/ theory/formula/technology/issue*
The truth/the answer/This proves/I will prove *The fact is that/I am sure/certain/ convinced Obviously/Of course/It is clear that* *It is accepted that/We all know that*	*The evidence suggests that / From the data it seems probable that / It is likely that* *It seems/appears from the evidence that* *The data strongly suggests that*
wonderful/lovely/pretty/fantastic/ terrible/absolutely	Do not use subjective and emotional adjectives.
Nowadays/These days/Recently/At the moment	*Currently/Over the last few/Since*
Don't use direct questions. E.g. *What should we do about it?*	Use indirect questions. E.g. *The main question to ask is what society should do to . . .* *The main challenge is . . .*

I believe/Personally, I think that/In my experience	*I argue that/I have suggested that*
I must admit that/As far as I'm concerned	*The studies show that/The research supports the idea that*
I cannot deny that	*A possible solution would be to*
We should/shouldn't/must/mustn't	*Further research on X would provide further insights into*

Key points

1 Producing successful academic writing does not mean using complex sentences and long words – it means being clear and precise.

2 Use logical order of content to structure your assignment rather than relying on linking and signposting language.

3 It's not up to the tutor to understand what you meant to say, but to mark what you did say.

4 Think of your assignment as telling your reader an important, interesting, evidenced and persuasive story.

For more advice, see *Writing for University* in this series.

 FROM ENGLISH LANGUAGE TEST TO UNIVERSITY SUCCESS

End comments

I hope this book has helped you become more aware of the differences between the demands of English language tests and those of university study. Your academic tutors will not be testing your grammatical knowledge, and they will not expect you to produce top-level assignments straight away. What they do want to see is that you are steadily developing your subject knowledge by thinking deeply about it, and that you are trying to express your ideas clearly and precisely.

If there is one thing you take away from reading this book, it should be that English language tests ask you to describe the *what*, whereas university study is about discussing the *why*.

References

Emeihe, E. V., Nwankwo, E. I., Ajegbile, M. D., Olaboye, J. A. and Maha, C. C. (2024). Revolutionizing drug delivery systems: Nanotechnology-based approaches for targeted therapy. *International Journal of Life Science Research Archive*, 7(1), 40–58.

Hammelman, C., Shoffner, E., Cruzat, M. and Lee, S. (2022). Assembling agroecological socio-natures: A political ecology analysis of urban and peri-urban agriculture in Rosario, Argentina. *Agriculture and Human Values*, 39(1), 371–83.

International Federation of the Phonographic Industry (ifpi) Global Music Report 2025, p. 4. Available at https://www.ifpi.org/wp-content/uploads/2024/03/GMR2025_SOTI.pdf (Accessed 25 April 2025.)

Murray, N. (2016). *Standards of English in higher education: Issues, challenges and strategies*. Cambridge University Press.

Selwyn, N. (2024). The modern classroom chair: Exploring the 'coercive design' of contemporary schooling. *Power and Education*, 16(1), 63–77.

Urban Farming Global Market Report (2025), p. 1. Available at https://www.thebusinessresearchcompany.com/report/urban-farming-global-market-report (Accessed 12 May 2025.)

Index